This book is dedicated to Dr. Bonnie Henry, a great germ hunter
who has inspired me to be a better disease detective. —J.G.

To all the Owlkids illustrators who inspired me to draw
when I was younger. —J.H.

Owlkids Books acknowledges the financial support of the Canada Council for the Arts, the
Ontario Arts Council, the Government of Canada through the Canada Book Fund (CBF),
and the Government of Ontario through the Ontario Media Development Corporation's Book
Initiative for our publishing activities.

Published in Canada by
Owlkids Books Inc.
10 Lower Spadina Avenue
Toronto, ON M5V 2Z2

Published in the United States by
Owlkids Books Inc.
1700 Fourth Street
Berkeley, CA 94710

Library and Archives Canada Cataloguing in Publication

Gardy, Jennifer, author
       It's catching : the infectious world of germs and microbes / written
by Jennifer Gardy ; illustrated by Josh Holinaty.

Includes index.
ISBN 978-1-77147-001-8 (bound).--ISBN 978-1-77147-053-7 (pbk.)

       1. Bacteria--Juvenile literature. 2. Microorganisms--Juvenile literature.
I. Holinaty, Josh, illustrator II. Title.

QR74.8.G37 2014   j579.3   C2013-904512-0

Library of Congress Control Number: 2013949230

Design: Barb Kelly

Manufactured in Shenzhen, Guangdong, China, in April 2015, by WKT Co. Ltd.
Job #15CB0173

B   C   D   E   F

Publisher of Chirp, chickaDEE and OWL
www.owlkidsbooks.com

IT'S CATCHING

THE INFECTIOUS WORLD OF GERMS AND MICROBES

BY JENNIFER GARDY, PhD
ILLUSTRATED BY JOSH HOLINATY

Owlkids Books

Contents

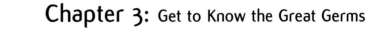

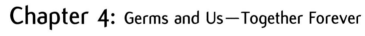

INTRODUCTION
I'm a Disease Detective

My name is Jennifer, and I love germs. No, really—
I do! But before you start thinking I'm a bit weird
(even though it's true), you should know that I DON'T
love getting sick and feeling like a piano just fell on
my head. What I DO love is studying the wonderful
world of microbes and figuring out how and why they
make us sick.

I'm a disease detective. When an outbreak of an
infectious disease happens, I'm on the scene. I've spent
over fifteen years studying the bacteria, viruses, and
other bugs that make us sick—learning what makes
them dangerous, how they spread from person to
person, and what sorts of tools can keep us healthy.

Just like a crime scene investigator, I use
evidence—things like interviews, fingerprints,
and DNA analysis—to figure out what happened.
There are a few differences, of course.

I don't interview criminals. Instead, I talk to the
people who got sick.

The fingerprints I analyze? They're not real
human fingerprints—they're DNA fingerprints.

And the DNA I study doesn't come from
people—it comes from germs like influenza,
measles, and tuberculosis.

Hi, my name is Jennifer, and I LOVE germs!

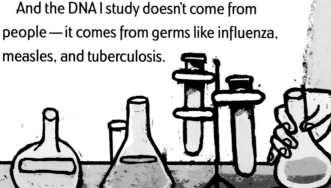

This book is a collection of some of the neat things I've learned on the job:

from the pudding that launched a whole scientific field

and the parasite that can take over our minds

to the man who drank a flask full of bacteria to prove a point (and won a Nobel Prize along the way!).

You'll see how germs use all sorts of clever tricks to make people sick, and how humans have been able to stay one step ahead.

You'll also learn how germs have shaped the course of human history, influencing everything from our own DNA to the sewers running beneath our streets.

Scientists believe that all life — you, me, plants, animals, dinosaurs, and all the great germs — began four billion years ago with a special cell called a microbe. Since then, there have been more microbes on Earth than people, plants, and animals combined! With all these millions of marvelous microbes to study, we'd better get a move on.

GRAB YOUR LAB NOTEBOOK and a microscope, if you've got one handy. It's time to get to know the great germs!

Meet the
MICROBES!

All germs are microbes, but
not all microbes are germs.

Before you can understand germs, you need to understand microbes. A microbe is a very small living thing. In fact, the word "microbe" comes from the Greek *mikros*, meaning "very small," and *bios*, meaning "life." Microbiology is the study of microbes, and scientists who study microbes are called microbiologists.

Most microbes are friendly, but a very small number can cause disease. Scientists call these unfriendly microbes pathogens — but many people use the nickname germs. The illnesses caused by pathogens are called infectious diseases.

Microbes are everywhere. The hands you're using to hold this book? Covered in microbes! The air you're breathing right now? Teeming with microbes! The lake or ocean you went swimming in that one awesome summer? Chock full of microbes!

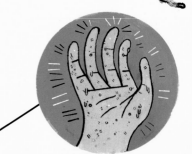

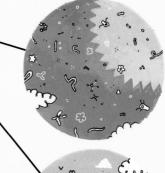

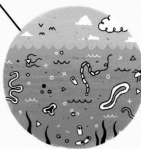

MICROBES
very small living things

→ **MICROBIOLOGY**
study of microbes

↳ **MICROBIOLOGISTS**
scientists who study microbes

→ **MICROBES** ——→ **PATHOGENS**
friendly, but some   the unfriendly microbes
can cause disease

↳ **INFECTIOUS DISEASES**
illnesses caused by pathogens

No matter where on Earth scientists look, they find microbes. There are so many microbes that if you collected them all and put them on a scale, they would weigh about 500 billion metric tons — more than all of the animals, plants, and people on Earth put together!

And if you think weighing microbes is hard, forget about counting them! Even if you counted one microbe every second, it would take you over three million years just to count the ones in your body.

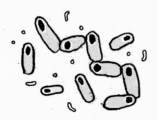

Roll Call!
Discovering micro-what lives micro-where

Your teacher takes attendance to find out who's in your classroom. Microbiologists can do the same thing to identify all the microbes living in a particular environment, like your nose, the soil, or even your pet. This environment is called the microbiome. Taking a microbial roll call is not as easy as calling out names, though! It requires a specialized form of DNA analysis that was invented only recently. In fact, it was only in 2012 that scientists were able to make a list of the many microbes living in the different parts of the human body.

Microbial fingerprints

Each of us has a unique community of microbes living in and around our body, and we leave these microbes everywhere we go, just as we do our fingerprints. In an experiment called the Home Microbiome Project, scientists sampled the microbes in a house before and after people moved in. Before the move, each room in the house had its own distinctive microbiome. After people moved in, the house's microbes were replaced with the ones carried by the new inhabitants.

Sometimes, we even leave real microbial fingerprints behind! Microbiologists recently discovered that they could tell which computer keyboard belonged to a particular individual by comparing the microbiome on the keys to the microbiome on an individual's fingers!

Secrets of the
INVISIBLE WORLD

Microbes are invisible to the naked eye, but when we zoom in for a closer look, we can see their world is a pretty busy place.

Pull a hair off your head. (You have about a hundred thousand of them—losing one won't hurt!) Take a close look at it. Pretty thin, isn't it? Your hair is about 0.1 millimeters, or 100 microns, in diameter. How does the size of our miniature microbial friends compare?

Parasites are the biggest of the microbes. The average parasite cell measures 10 microns, so you could fit ten across a single strand of hair. The smallest microbes? Viruses. The tiniest viruses known to scientists—parvoviruses—are so little you could fit five thousand of them across the width of one hair!

Zoom in

To actually see microbes, scientists need a microscope. The first microscope was believed to have been invented by Dutch lensmakers Hans and Zacharias Janssen in 1595. This invention was later improved by Italian scientist Galileo Galilei in 1609—the same basic design is still in use today. These machines—called optical microscopes or light microscopes—illuminate a sample from underneath. Light shines through the sample and passes through a series of glass lenses that act like magnifying glasses, making the sample appear larger.

Where it all began

Antonie van Leeuwenhoek (1632–1723) (say "van LAY-ven-hook") is often called the father of microbiology. His work with microscopes helped uncover the microbial world. He used microscopes he built himself to study water samples from lakes, rain, and snow. In these samples, he observed wiggly little creatures he called "animalcules." His drawings of these "little animals" were so detailed that centuries later, scientists were able to determine exactly which types of microbes he had observed back in 1674.

One ticket to Microbe City, please!

If you were to zoom in on one of van Leeuwenhoek's samples, you'd see a tremendous amount of activity—a drop of pond water might seem as busy as a big city! In fact, there are a lot of similarities between the way we humans live and the way our microbial friends do.

In our cities:

- Some people live alone, while others stick together in groups.
- Some folks prefer the outdoors, while others like to stay inside.
- Some people love to move around, zooming along our busy streets, while others prefer to stay put.
- Some parts of the city are quite busy, while other neighborhoods are much quieter.

In Microbe City, the same things are true:

- Some organisms hang out on their own, while others are always found in pairs or larger groups.
- Some species can thrive in any environment, while others need to get inside a human cell to survive.
- Some microbes are motile (able to move)—they use tadpole-like tails to swim around—while others are stuck in one place.
- Some environments (like water or soil) are home to millions and millions of microbes, while other environments (like our own blood) host very few of them.

CULTURE CLUB

How do you work with something too small to see? Jelly!

To work with microbes, scientists have to grow enough microbial cells to see and touch. This is called culturing the microbes. Culturing doesn't involve going to the museum! It just takes a little food, a little warmth, and a little waiting.

Way to grow!

Microbes are cultured on agar plates. These are Petri dishes (small round plates) filled with a jelly-like material (called agar), only this jelly doesn't taste like strawberry or lime or orange. Bacteria don't enjoy the same food we humans do—they prefer gelatin made of stinky things like meat juice and blood.

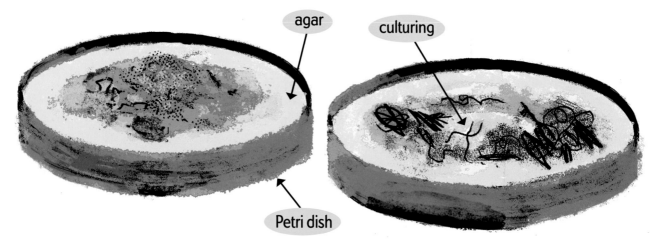

agar

culturing

Petri dish

The first step in culturing is to collect a sample that contains our invisible microbes of interest—maybe a drop of pond water or a cotton swab we've put in our nose—and spread it all over the agar plate. Next, we place the plate in a warm incubator. Most microbes are happiest at 98.6°F (37°C)—the same temperature as warm-blooded animals, including humans. After a few days to a few weeks (some microbes grow fast, while others grow slowly), the microbes will have multiplied so many times that we can see colonies on the Petri dish. Each of these colonies (which usually look like shiny, sticky mush) contains millions of microbial cells—enough for any experiments we might want to do.

The PUDDING that saved science

It was a hot German summer in the 1880s, and Walther Hesse was MAD! Every day Walther would set out Petri dishes full of beef-flavored gelatin, hoping to catch and culture microbes. But when he went back to check hours later, he'd always find that the gelatin had melted in the summer heat. Walther vented his frustration to his wife, Angelina, whose puddings and jams didn't seem to melt, even though her kitchen was just as hot as his lab. That's when she let him in on the kitchen secret that would change science: agar! Agar is a powder from certain types of algae that acts like a super-gelatin. The next day, Walther was overjoyed to discover that his wife's agar had worked and his plates were still solid!

Still used today

This simple bit of kitchen chemistry allowed microbiologists to reliably grow bacteria on solid material, making them much easier to study. Who would have thought that a dessert recipe would change the course of microbiology?

NOT FOR EVERYONE

Not all microbes can be cultured. In fact, we know how to grow only a tiny fraction of the world's microbes in the lab. The rest are unculturable. But we know they're there thanks to DNA analysis.

RAISE YOUR OWN PET MOLD

Want to culture your own microbes? It's easy! In fact, you've probably already done it if you've ever forgotten your lunchbox at school for a few days. When you opened it up, the food inside probably looked pretty furry, right? That's mold — a type of fungus that grows on organic matter such as bread or fruit.

To grow your own mold, you will need:

- 4 clear plastic containers or jars with lids
- 4 food samples — a piece of bread and a few different fruits and vegetables
- a safe place to store your mold cultures for a few days

1. Put one food sample in each container. Leave the containers open overnight so that mold in the environment will land on the food.

2. The next morning, put a lid on each container and store the containers in a safe place.

3. Every day, check the mold growth in each container. If you have a notebook, describe what type of mold you observe. (Is it green? Is it brown? Is it wildly fluffy or just sort of fuzzy?) Also note how big the mold colonies are.

4. You can stop the experiment whenever you think the samples look too yucky. Make sure to clean the containers in hot, soapy water after you've thrown your samples out.

Germs 101

A germ is a microbe that can cause disease in a living thing.

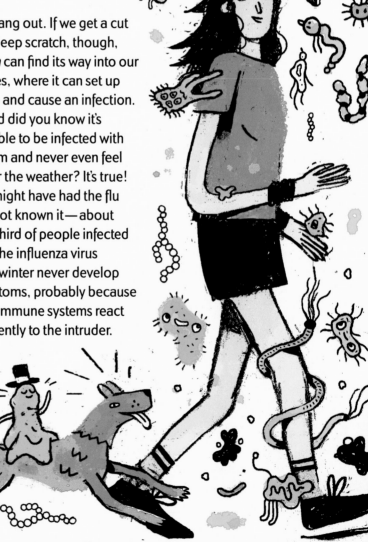

Whether they are viruses, bacteria, fungi, or parasites, germs can take lots of different forms. But—and this is a pretty big "but"—these gross little guys don't always make you sick! Many of us carry germs around on our skin and in our noses all the time without becoming ill.

Most germs are what we call opportunistic pathogens—they co-exist peacefully with humans but can cause disease if they're given the chance. For example, the bacterium known as *Staphylococcus aureus* is found on most people's skin (yep, including yours), where it's happy to just hang out. If we get a cut or a deep scratch, though, *Staph* can find its way into our bodies, where it can set up camp and cause an infection.

And did you know it's possible to be infected with a germ and never even feel under the weather? It's true! You might have had the flu and not known it—about one-third of people infected with the influenza virus each winter never develop symptoms, probably because their immune systems react differently to the intruder.

Germs may not always make us sick, but when they do, they don't just cause infectious diseases. Germs have been linked to conditions ranging from obesity to heart disease. They are even known to cause certain types of cancer. A bacterial or viral infection can cause our own cells to malfunction. When these cells start growing out of control, the result is a tumor.

Understanding how germs work and why they make us sick is a big part of being a microbiologist. So grab your lab notebook—we're going to germ school!

Start Your Engines!

When scientists want to describe the relationship between different germs, they use taxonomy.

The germ taxonomy

Taxonomy is a big word for some simple rules about naming things. To understand taxonomy, let's think about vehicles. They fall into a few broad categories—cars, vans, motorcycles, trucks. These vehicles are all similar—they have wheels—but they're also very different.

Germs fall into a few broad categories, too: viruses, bacteria, fungi, and parasites. We call these categories domains. Just like the forms of transport, the four germ domains have many differences—different looks, different life cycles, and different ways of making people sick.

Makes and models

In the automotive world, each car company offers several models. You might drive a Speedmaster Z3000, while your friend has a Speedmaster X100—same make, different models. In the bacterial world, the equivalent terms are genus and species. There are genera (that's the fancy plural of "genus") like *Escherichia* or *Salmonella* or *Plasmodium*, each of which can contain tens or hundreds of individual species, like *Escherichia coli* or *Salmonella typhimurium* or *Plasmodium falciparum*.

I'll take the red convertible, please

When you bought your Speedmaster Z3000, you had to make a few decisions. Red or black? Convertible or hardtop? Within a single species, microbes have options, too. These options usually mean differences in how contagious a germ is or what type of disease it causes. We call slightly different versions of the same species strains.

VIRUSES

Viruses may be the smallest of the germs, but these teeny-tiny troublemakers cause some of the most contagious diseases on Earth!

Viruses look like small geometrical capsules. The hard outer shell of a virus is made up of proteins that fit together like puzzle pieces, while inside the shell is its DNA — the genetic instructions the virus uses to make copies of itself. Unlike other microbes, viruses can't reproduce on their own — in order to replicate, a virus has to get inside one of our cells and take over its protein-making machinery.

How do viruses make you sick?

If someone broke into your house and started playing with all your stuff and eating all your food, you'd be pretty angry, right? Well, when a virus barges into one of your cells, the cell gets mad! In fact, when you're sick with a virus, most of your symptoms aren't caused by the virus itself. Instead, they're the side effects of your body's fight against the tiny invader.

When your body is confronted with a virus, different types of immune cells move throughout your body to hunt for the intruder. The cells "talk" to each other, using special molecules called cytokines to say things like, "Send help! I see some viruses over here!" The only problem is that immune cells have pretty loud "voices"— sometimes other cells overhear the conversation and join the fight by becoming inflamed or producing mucus. That's what causes the symptoms of a viral infection.

So the next time you're in bed with a cold and a big box of tissues, take comfort in the fact that your drippy nose means your body is doing its best to get healthy again!

BACTERIA

Our bodies contain ten times as many bacterial cells as human cells. Most are harmless, but a few have some not-so-nice tricks up their sleeves.

Bacteria are single-celled organisms that come in a range of shapes. If you can draw it, there's probably a bacterium shaped like it! There are spherical bacteria called cocci, rod-shaped bacteria called bacilli, and all sorts of other bacteria—from squiggly coils to squares to stars.

One...two...four...many

Unlike viruses, bacteria can reproduce on their own through a process called binary fission. One bacterial cell divides into two, then each of those two cells divides again, then each of those four divides again, and so on. The bacterium *Escherichia coli* (*E. coli*, to its friends) takes about twenty minutes to divide. So after one hour, one *E. coli* cell has turned into eight. After only six and a half hours, there will be over a MILLION bacteria! It's easy to see why a bacterial infection can quickly turn dangerous.

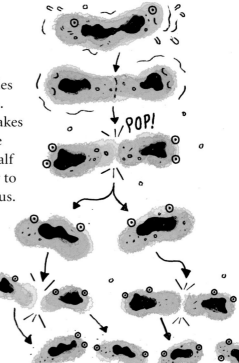

What makes some bacteria germs?

Just as there are many shapes of bacteria, there are many ways in which pathogenic bacteria can cause disease. The symptoms of some bacterial infections are the result of our immune systems being hard at work. That achy ear infection? It's your body fighting off an invader like *Streptococcus pneumoniae*.

Other bacterial pathogens produce toxins, which are poisonous compounds that can damage our own cells. *Vibrio cholerae*, the bacterium that causes the diarrheal disease cholera, is one of these. It makes a protein called cholera toxin, which causes our intestines to release huge amounts of water—as much as 0.5 gallons (2 liters) every hour!

FUNGI

Some fungi are fun guys.
Others...not so much.

Like mushroom pepperoni pizza? Each slice has three different types of fungi! The dough rises thanks to the yeast *Saccharomyces cerevisiae*. The pepperoni's flavor comes from a mold called *Penicillium*. And the mushrooms were probably *Agaricus bisporus*.

Most of the 1.5 million species of fungi estimated to exist on Earth are friendly. Many fungi actually help us fight disease! Since the 1940s, scientists have been harvesting natural antibiotics from fungi, including penicillin (see page 46). Thanks to fungi, many deadly bacterial infections are now curable.

The not-so-fun guys

Still, a few fungi can cause disease by growing out of control. Have you ever had itchy, flaky skin between your toes? That's athlete's foot, and almost two-thirds of us will have it at some point in our lives. Fortunately, this fungal skin infection is easily treated.

Fungal infections in other parts of our bodies can be more serious, especially in people with weak immune systems. Many fungal diseases, like aspergillosis or coccidioidomycosis, start when you inhale a small fungal particle called a spore. The spore settles in the lung, where it begins to grow and divide. The ball of fungus grows larger and larger and can eventually make it difficult to breathe.

HUMUNGOUS FUNGUS

In 1998, scientists in Oregon discovered a colony of the fungus Armillaria ostoyae measuring nearly 4 square miles (10 square kilometers). That's 1,665 football fields full of fantastic fungus!

PARASITES

Parasites exploit other species in order to survive. This can come at a deadly cost to the unsuspecting host.

Parasites come in many shapes and sizes. Some, like *Entamoeba*, are single cells. A few, like bedbugs or lice, look like small insects. Others, including certain tapeworms, can grow to 65 feet (20 meters) in length — longer than a school bus! So what do these tiny cells, creepy-crawly bugs, and giant tapeworms have in common? To reproduce, they have to get inside the right host, and once there they scavenge nutrients and set up a cozy home — all at the host's expense.

The stuff nightmares are made of

If there were a Big Book of Bad Bugs, the stuff about parasites would take up a lot of pages. While most germs are content to cause a fever here, a little diarrhea there, parasites cause some of the scariest and weirdest diseases around! Happily for us humans, most of the parasites behind the creepiest of conditions are found in animals. There's *Leucochloridium paradoxum*, a flatworm that infects a snail's eye tentacles, stretching them and changing their color to make them look like long caterpillars! And then there's *Ribeiroia*, a group of worms that can cause frogs to grow extra legs! And don't forget the *Gordiacea*. These long, thin worms control crickets' behavior by reprogramming the bugs' brains!

Parasites are for people, too

Just because we're not snails or frogs or crickets doesn't mean we're safe, though — there are plenty of human diseases caused by parasites. From the tiny amoeba that can infiltrate our brains to the roundworm that can cause our legs to swell up to many times their normal size, these unwelcome guests can trigger many diseases.

Get to Know the Great Germs!

There are thousands of germs in the world, and it's somebody's job to keep track of them all!

In 1948, the United Nations created the World Health Organization—WHO to its friends. Headquartered in Geneva, Switzerland, WHO is tasked with monitoring all the diseases in the world.

Every year, WHO publishes a report describing the global morbidity and mortality rates for all the diseases it tracks. Morbidity is a measure of how many people got sick, while mortality refers to how many of those people died. In the developed world, morbidity and mortality rates due to infectious diseases are low.

In other parts of the world, where people can't see a doctor or a nurse as easily as they can in North America or Europe, germs are a much bigger problem.

And how many germs do the folks at WHO have to keep on top of? Lots! There are almost two thousand infectious diseases that make humans sick. In fact, it's a true A-to-Z! The Great Germ Alphabet starts with acanthamebiasis and goes all the way through to zygomycosis. Meeting all of them would take some time. But a few names rise to the top. Here they are—the greatest germs of them all.

WHO =
WORLD HEALTH
ORGANIZATION

Just how common are these great germs? There are 7 billion people on the planet Earth. In one year:

- 2.8 million people will become infected with HIV, the virus that causes AIDS.
- 9 million people will get Dengue fever, a virus spread by tropical mosquitos.
- 27.2 million people will be covered in an itchy red rash from the measles virus.
- 241.4 million people will be infected by the parasite causing malaria.
- 446.8 million people will get a respiratory infection like bronchitis or pneumonia.
- 4.6 billion bouts of diarrhea will occur. That means about half of the world's population will have diarrhea once every year.

That's a lot of germs. So many, in fact, that it's virtually certain that all 7 billion of us will get sick at least once a year!

Great Germs, by the Numbers

If you want to be a great germologist, you'll need to learn to recognize the signs and symptoms of different diseases, describe how they transmit, and understand how dangerous they are. Each of the great germs that follows will have a card just like this one.

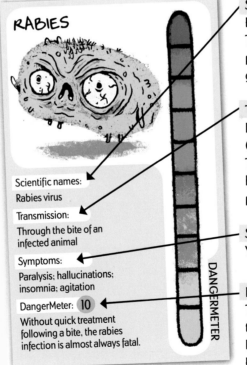

RABIES

Scientific names:
Rabies virus

Transmission:
Through the bite of an infected animal

Symptoms:
Paralysis; hallucinations; insomnia; agitation

DangerMeter: 10
Without quick treatment following a bite, the rabies infection is almost always fatal.

DANGERMETER

Scientific name:
Every germ has a name. This section will tell you the proper name for each of the great germs.

Transmission:
Does this cootie like to fly? Or is it found in a cow pie? Transmission describes how the germ spreads from person to person.

Symptoms:
You know you're sick when...

DangerMeter:
The DangerMeter score tells you how bad each bug is on a scale of 1 to 10. Being deadly and/or easily transmissible earns a high score here.

THE COMMON COLD—
The No-No Your Nose Knows

The common cold is uncommonly unique. While most infectious diseases are caused by only one germ, colds are caused by hundreds. The usual culprit is rhinovirus (Greek for "nose virus"), but many other viruses can cause the runny nose, sneezing, and coughing of a "cold."

Sniffles AGAIN?!

When we get infected with a virus, our body's immune system usually produces antibodies that stay inside us for years. These special proteins will recognize a particular virus and are ready to pounce on that germ if it ever returns. So why do we keep getting sick with colds? Shouldn't our antibodies be protecting us?

In the case of a rhinovirus, the answer is a snotty, sneezy "no." Our bodies will make rhinovirus antibodies only about half of the time. Even then, because there are at least ninety-nine strains of rhinovirus, the antibodies made against one strain won't help us fight off others.

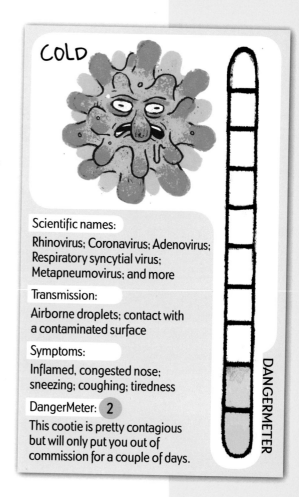

COLD

Scientific names:
Rhinovirus; Coronavirus; Adenovirus; Respiratory syncytial virus; Metapneumovirus; and more

Transmission:
Airborne droplets; contact with a contaminated surface

Symptoms:
Inflamed, congested nose; sneezing; coughing; tiredness

DangerMeter: 2
This cootie is pretty contagious but will only put you out of commission for a couple of days.

DANGERMETER

FACT

WHITHER THE WEATHER?

You can't catch a cold from being cold. Sure, more colds happen in winter, but that's because more people spend time indoors—where they can trade viruses with other people—not because they forgot to put on mitts!

NAME THAT GERM

Why is a cold called a cold?
Why not a hot? Or George?
In the sixteenth century, people noticed that the symptoms of a cold—like a red, runny nose—looked a lot like the symptoms caused by exposure to cold weather. The name "cold" stuck, even after people realized that colds had nothing to do with the weather.

Crazy cold concoctions

Coming down with a cold? Chances are you've heard about a hundred different suggestions for fighting it off. Here are some of the wackier ones.

WEAR WET SOCKS. Some folks claim that going to sleep in soaking socks stimulates circulation, relieving congestion and helping your immune cells reach the site of infection.

EAT SOME CHOCOLATE. Theobromine, one of the compounds in dark chocolate, is said to soothe the reflex that makes you feel like coughing.

CHOW DOWN ON CURRY. Fenugreek, a spice often used in South Asian cooking, is thought to have antiviral properties.

LISTEN TO JAZZ MUSIC. A trumpet a day keeps the doctor away? It has been claimed that listening to thirty minutes of jazz music every day boosts levels of a special germ-fighting antibody called immunoglobulin A.

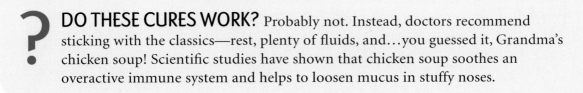

? DO THESE CURES WORK? Probably not. Instead, doctors recommend sticking with the classics—rest, plenty of fluids, and…you guessed it, Grandma's chicken soup! Scientific studies have shown that chicken soup soothes an overactive immune system and helps to loosen mucus in stuffy noses.

INFLUENZA— The Flu in You

Spies are masters of disguise, constantly changing their appearance so they aren't recognized. A dye job here, a new mustache there, and sometimes even more dramatic changes—going bald or gaining lots of weight.

Turns out, influenza is the secret agent of the virus world. Sometimes it makes small changes to its appearance and other times drastic alterations—all so that it can continue to infect humans year after year. Why all the costume changes? Because if influenza didn't evolve so quickly, it wouldn't stand a chance against our impressive immune systems.

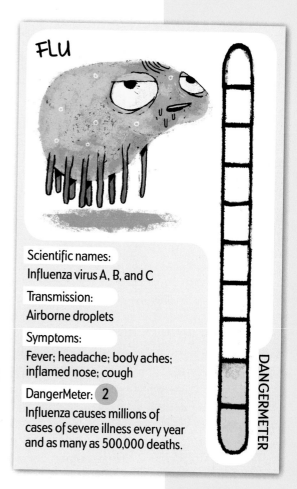

FLU

Scientific names:
Influenza virus A, B, and C

Transmission:
Airborne droplets

Symptoms:
Fever; headache; body aches; inflamed nose; cough

DangerMeter: 2
Influenza causes millions of cases of severe illness every year and as many as 500,000 deaths.

DANGERMETER

Fooled again!

Every year, as many as one billion people around the world get sick with flu—that's one in every seven people! Almost all of those people will develop antibodies against the particular virus they caught, which will protect them from getting that type of flu again. If the flu virus never changed, it would take only a few short years for everyone in the world to become infected and develop protective antibodies. When the virus ran out of people to infect (we call them susceptible hosts), it would die out.

Instead, influenza changes its disguise every year. The antibodies we made against earlier infections don't recognize the new virus, and this airborne antagonist is free to spread.

KNOW YOUR COOTIES?

Colds and flus both spread through the air and wreak havoc in your nose and throat. But they are caused by totally different viruses. How do you know which you've got? If it came on quickly, it's probably flu. Flus also make you feel worse than colds do — feverish, achy, and nauseated instead of just a little grumpy and sniffly.

Look into my crystal ball

Twice a year, the disease detectives at WHO make a very important prediction. They have to guess what "disguise" the influenza virus will be wearing in the next few months so that they can produce the correct vaccine to protect people around the world. Making a vaccine takes many months of laboratory work, so WHO's scientists must choose their recipe well ahead of time—in February for the northern hemisphere's winter and in September for winter south of the equator.

How do they know what to put in the vaccine? They have a worldwide network of research laboratories that are constantly collecting flu samples from doctors' offices and hospitals. The scientists examine the samples using experimental techniques that give them a sneak peek at the virus's disguises. Will this winter be a fake mustache, a silly pair of glasses, or a new haircut? Who knows? WHO knows!

FACT

ONE SHOT TO STOP THE SNOT?

Scientists are working on a universal flu vaccine. Instead of trying to unmask the flu virus's shifting disguise, the universal vaccine will recognize those parts of the virus that don't change very often. If researchers are successful, the World Health Organization won't have to guess which flu shot recipe to use each year—one shot will protect people against many different strains of flu!

FOOD POISONING—
When Food Bites Back!

Food poisoning is the catchall name for a variety of diseases caused mostly by bacteria and viruses (although some plants, algae, fungi, and fish also produce toxins that can send your tummy into a tizzy).

Nobody knows exactly how common food poisoning is because when we have an upset tummy, most of us chalk it up to bad shrimp or some funky milk and just wait it out without seeing a doctor. We do know, though, that food poisoning is easily prevented.

Wash up!

The germs that cause food poisoning usually get into our food system when poop touches something we will eventually eat—a bird poops on a field of lettuce, or a meat processing plant gets too unclean. If the food is handled properly—washed before use, cooked to the right temperature, and kept in the refrigerator—these germs are killed before they ever have a chance to make us ill. But if we skip these steps, or if we fail to properly wash our work surfaces and cooking tools, we run the risk of getting sick.

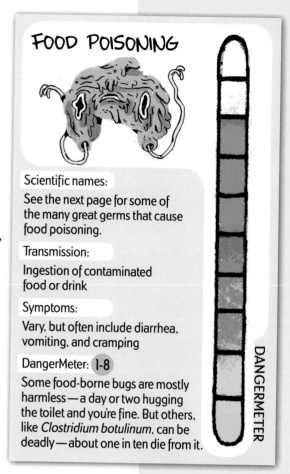

FOOD POISONING

Scientific names:
See the next page for some of the many great germs that cause food poisoning.

Transmission:
Ingestion of contaminated food or drink

Symptoms:
Vary, but often include diarrhea, vomiting, and cramping

DangerMeter: 1-8
Some food-borne bugs are mostly harmless—a day or two hugging the toilet and you're fine. But others, like *Clostridium botulinum*, can be deadly—about one in ten die from it.

DANGERMETER

FACT

STOMACH FLU, STOMACH WHO?

People often say they've come down with the "stomach flu," but this flu isn't caused by influenza. What we call "stomach flu" is a disease whose real name is viral gastroenteritis, which is caused by viruses like norovirus and rotavirus.

Know the rude dudes in your foods

There are hundreds of organisms that can cause food poisoning. Here are a few of the most common culprits, and a few of the tricks they use to make you sick.

Campylobacter jejuni

This bacterium loves raw poultry and unpasteurized milk. It produces a toxin that can damage the cells in your intestine.

Clostridium perfringens

Nicknamed "the cafeteria bacteria," this bug likes to grow in starchy food prepared in large batches and then left to sit out.

Salmonella

Found most often in eggs and meats, *Salmonella* bacteria are also spread by reptiles kept as pets. Wash your hands after petting that turtle!

Escherichia coli O157:H7

The "hamburger disease" bacterium got its nickname because it's often found in undercooked ground beef. It produces a toxin that breaks down the delicate lining of your gut.

Listeria monocytogenes

Normally, infection by this bacterium causes an unpleasant but uncomplicated bout of food poisoning. But watch out—if *Listeria* gets past the gut and into the blood, it can reach the brain, causing a deadly condition called meningitis.

Clostridium botulinum

Found in jams and preserves that weren't prepared properly, this bad bug produces one of the deadliest toxins on Earth—it enters our nerve cells and paralyzes them. Believe it or not, this same toxin is used in cosmetic surgery. Marketed as Botox, it's injected into people's foreheads to make wrinkles disappear!

RABIES —
Putting the Wild in Wildlife

Rabies, one of the deadliest viruses in the world, lives in the saliva of an infected mammal. Dogs, raccoons, skunks, and bats are common carriers. When a rabid animal bites a human, the virus enters the muscle tissue. From there, it creeps up into the nerve fibers — the wiring that helps that muscle to move. Eventually it reaches the central nervous system — the brain and the spinal cord — where it can spread to nerves throughout the body, causing paralysis and frightening psychological symptoms, like hydrophobia, an extreme fear of drinking water!

Until the late nineteenth century, every case of human rabies was fatal. Then, in 1885, the French chemist and microbiologist Louis Pasteur made a breakthrough: he created a rabies vaccine that could be used not only to prevent rabies but also to stop the disease from developing in someone who has just been bitten. If given quickly enough after a bite, the rabies vaccine is 100 percent effective at preventing the fatal disease.

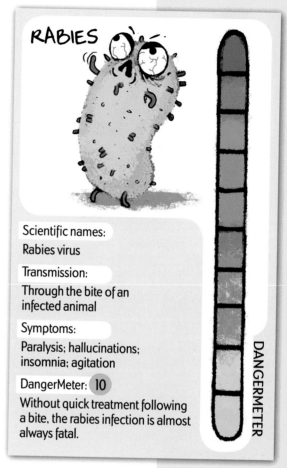

RABIES

Scientific names:
Rabies virus

Transmission:
Through the bite of an infected animal

Symptoms:
Paralysis; hallucinations; insomnia; agitation

DangerMeter: 10
Without quick treatment following a bite, the rabies infection is almost always fatal.

DANGERMETER

A rare case

Only a handful of people have survived rabies without receiving the vaccine after being infected. The first known survivor, Jeanna Giese, was bitten by a bat in Wisconsin in 2004. She developed rabies symptoms a month later. Doctors speculated that if her central nervous system could be temporarily shut down, the rabies virus might not be able to hijack her brain and cause death. They put her into a medically induced coma for six days—long enough, they believed, for her immune system to fight off the deadly virus. It worked! Jeanna is now a happy and healthy adult, and the treatment her doctors developed has saved other victims, too.

Snack pack prevents rabies attack!

Some countries have almost completely eliminated rabies by vaccinating wildlife. Because it's impossible to give a rabies shot to every animal in the wilderness, the vaccine is placed into a small plastic pouch coated with food crumbs, called a bait. The baits are dropped from helicopters or placed by wildlife officers in areas frequented by wild mammals. When an animal munches on the bait, the plastic pouch containing the liquid vaccine bursts, giving the hungry critter a dose of the rabies vaccine.

MAYBE RABIES ISN'T SO BAD?

Humans have known about rabies for over four thousand years, but it was only in 2012 that scientists discovered the disease may not be as deadly as we thought. When they looked at the blood of people living in Peru's Amazon jungle, they found that one in ten had antibodies to the rabies virus. This suggested they had been infected at some point but never developed disease.

MALARIA—
Revenge of the Mosquitos

Malaria is a parasitic disease spread by mosquitos of the *Anopheles* genus. It occurs in almost all of the tropical countries around the equator, where warm temperatures and regular rainfall make perfect nurseries for baby mosquitos.

From bug to blood

Malaria has a pretty nifty life cycle. It begins when a female mosquito bites an infected human. When the mosquito sucks up some delicious human blood, tiny parasite cells come along for the ride. They multiply in the mosquito's gut and eventually make their way to the insect's spit glands.

When the bug bites another human, the parasites are injected into that person's blood (along with some bug spit). After a quick pit stop in the liver, the parasites catch a wave on the bloodstream, where they cruise around, bursting blood cells and causing trouble.

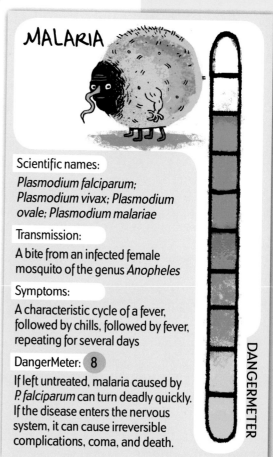

MALARIA

Scientific names:

Plasmodium falciparum; Plasmodium vivax; Plasmodium ovale; Plasmodium malariae

Transmission:

A bite from an infected female mosquito of the genus *Anopheles*

Symptoms:

A characteristic cycle of a fever, followed by chills, followed by fever, repeating for several days

DangerMeter: 8

If left untreated, malaria caused by *P. falciparum* can turn deadly quickly. If the disease enters the nervous system, it can cause irreversible complications, coma, and death.

DANGERMETER

MEET THE MOSQUITO

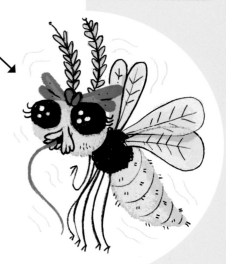

Name: *Anopheles*

Gender: Female. Female mosquitos need human blood to nourish their eggs. Males don't lay eggs, so they never develop the blood-sucking proboscis that females have.

Lifespan: Two to three weeks. But they make the most of it— females lay up to 150 eggs every two to three days!

Activity: These bugs prefer cool temperatures for biting— they're most active at nighttime.

Stop that bug!

Have you heard the saying "An ounce of prevention is worth a pound of cure"? It sure is true for malaria! Although malaria infections can be treated with drugs, it's easier to stop the mosquitos from biting in the first place. Some bite-banishing approaches are pretty simple, such as spraying insecticide inside homes where malaria is common. Others sound straight out of science fiction, like releasing genetically engineered sterile male mosquitos into the wild. Female mosquitos mate with these sterile decoys but don't produce offspring—and the population in the neighborhood quickly disappears.

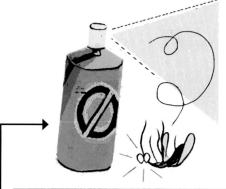

But one of the easiest ways to keep bugs from noshing on our tasty bits is to use mosquito netting. Mosquitos feed at night, so a mosquito net treated with insecticide and draped over the bed can prevent many bites. This simple solution has cut malaria rates in half in some places!

TREMENDOUS TONICS AND SUPER SHRUBS

The first-ever anti-malarial drug, quinine, was developed in the 1600s. Derived from the bark of the South American cinchona tree, quinine is a bitter-tasting chemical that's also found on your supermarket shelves — it's what gives tonic water its unique taste! The newest treatment of choice for malarial infections is artemisinin, which comes from the leaves of the wormwood plant. Although artemisinin has been used by Chinese herbalists since 200 BCE, scientists only discovered that it could cure malaria in 1972.

MEASLES—
Connect the Dots

What's a measle? Beats me. But when you're covered in 'em, you've got measles! Historians think the word "measle" comes from the fourteenth-century Dutch word *masel*, which means "blemish." That's a spot-on description for this cootie, which causes a blotchy red rash all over your body.

Measles used to be a common childhood illness, with almost every kid in the world quarantined in her bedroom, all covered in spots, at some point in her life. In 1963, a super-effective vaccine was developed, and measles rates plummeted...even though this virus is the most contagious in the world.

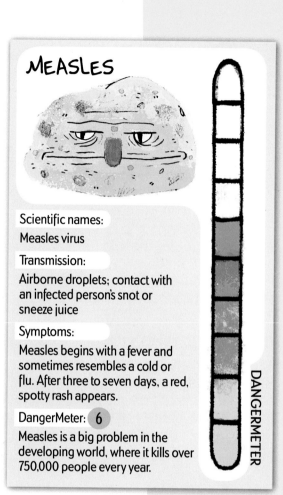

MEASLES

Scientific names:
Measles virus

Transmission:
Airborne droplets; contact with an infected person's snot or sneeze juice

Symptoms:
Measles begins with a fever and sometimes resembles a cold or flu. After three to seven days, a red, spotty rash appears.

DangerMeter: 6
Measles is a big problem in the developing world, where it kills over 750,000 people every year.

DANGERMETER

GREAT PLAGUES OF YESTERYEAR

In 165 BCE, the Antonine Plague spread through the Roman Empire, killing as much as one-third of the population. From the description recorded by the Roman historian Galen, some scientists think that measles was the culprit.

Doing the measles math

Epidemiologists—scientists who study the spread of disease—use a special number to describe how contagious a virus is. It's called the basic reproduction number, or R0 for short. It's complicated to calculate but simple to understand—it counts how many people one sick person is expected to infect over the course of his or her illness.

If I'm sick with a cold and I make two other people sick, the R0 of my virus is 2. Colds and seasonal flus typically have R0 values of around 1.5 to 2. The 1918 flu pandemic R0 was estimated to be 2 to 3, while diseases like polio and smallpox have R0 values of around 5 to 7.

Measles is the granddaddy of them all, though. Its R0 is thought to be around 12 to 18! Why is it so contagious? This virus likes to hang out in the cells lining your airways. Every cough or sneeze blasts tiny measles particles out of these cells and into the airways of anyone nearby.

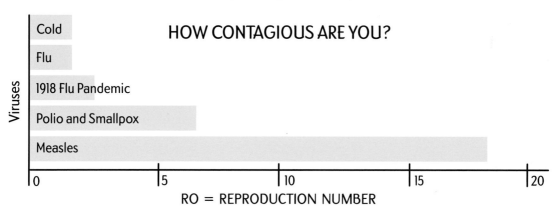

HOW CONTAGIOUS ARE YOU?

Viruses:
- Cold
- Flu
- 1918 Flu Pandemic
- Polio and Smallpox
- Measles

R0 = REPRODUCTION NUMBER
(axis: 0, 5, 10, 15, 20)

Thank you, David!

In 1954, two doctors in Boston were trying to develop a measles vaccine. To do their experiments, they needed a live virus, and for that, they needed a measles patient. They went to a local private school, where they met eleven-year-old David Edmonston, who was covered from head to toe in spots. The doctors swabbed David's throat, took a blood sample, and were able to culture his virus in their laboratory. They kept it alive and growing, and eventually (nine years later) the virus taken from David's throat was turned into the world's first measles vaccine. That strain, which is still used in vaccines today, was named Edmonston in honor of the young patient. David, we salute you!

HELLO, MY NAME IS:
EDMONSTON VACCINE

EBOLA—
Trouble in the Jungle

This great germ might be the scariest virus of all. It's classified as Biosafety Level 4 (BSL-4) and can be studied in only a handful of special laboratories around the world.

BIOSAFETY LEVELS

Every microbe is assigned a Biosafety Level (BSL) number, which tells scientists how dangerous the organism is. The levels are as follows:

BSL-1 These organisms don't cause disease in humans.

BSL-2 These organisms either cause mild disease in humans or are difficult for people to catch in a laboratory setting.

BSL-3 These germs are potentially deadly, but they can be treated.

BSL-4 These bad bugs are deadly, and there's no known treatment for infection.

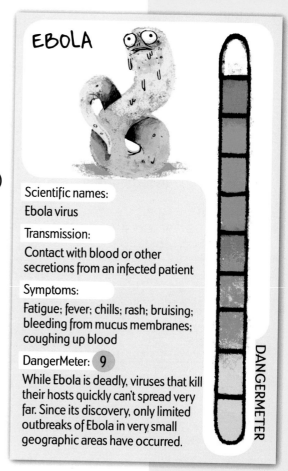

EBOLA

Scientific names:
Ebola virus

Transmission:
Contact with blood or other secretions from an infected patient

Symptoms:
Fatigue; fever; chills; rash; bruising; bleeding from mucus membranes; coughing up blood

DangerMeter: **9**
While Ebola is deadly, viruses that kill their hosts quickly can't spread very far. Since its discovery, only limited outbreaks of Ebola in very small geographic areas have occurred.

DANGERMETER

FACT

DANGER IN THE LABORATORY

Despite the precautions, laboratory accidents do occur. One of the scientists who first studied Ebola in 1976 became infected when he accidentally injected himself with the virus. He survived, but others haven't. Eight people have died in lab accidents caused by Ebola and its cousin, Marburg virus.

A mystery shaped like a question mark

In 1976, an unusual disease appeared in the village of Yambuku, Zaire (now the Democratic Republic of the Congo). Several patients in Yambuku's small hospital fell ill, first with fever and then with an unusual disease that caused them to vomit blood. At the same time, a village almost 500 miles (800 kilometers) away in Sudan was gripped by a similar outbreak. Between the two villages, over six hundred people were sick—in Yambuku, over 90 percent of those infected died.

The mystery disease didn't look like anything scientists had seen before, so WHO assembled a team of its best virus-hunters to study blood samples from the infected patients. When they looked at the samples using an electron microscope, they saw something unique—a virus shaped like a question mark! The new virus was named Ebola, after a river in the region where the disease first appeared.

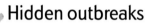

Hidden outbreaks

Since its discovery in 1976, Ebola has caused eighteen outbreaks, all in Africa. Scientists still aren't sure how these outbreaks start. They think that Ebola hides out in the jungles, in some sort of animal reservoir. This hypothesis is based on the fact that in some outbreaks, the first patient to get sick—known as the index case—had contact with monkeys, gorillas, chimpanzees, or bats. They haven't been able to confirm this hunch, though, and the search continues.

Suit up!

BSL-4 labs are the highest-security labs in the world, and getting into one isn't as simple as opening up a door. First, scientists enter a changeroom, where they take off their street clothes and put on scrubs, like the ones doctors wear. Next, they go into a second changeroom, where they don a special blue suit that covers their entire body. Made of a special tear-resistant plastic, the suit has its own air supply, much like a scuba suit. This allows the scientist inside to breathe clean air, even if there's a spill in the lab. Only after the air supply is turned on and the suit is checked for rips or holes is a scientist finally allowed to enter the heart of the BSL-4 lab.

TOXOPLASMOSIS—
The Germ That Loves Kitties

Toxoplasma gondii—the parasite that causes toxoplasmosis—loves cats. I love cats, too, but *T. gondii* REALLY loves them. It wants nothing more than to live inside a nice, warm kitty, happily reproducing in Fluffy's intestines.

When an infected cat visits the litterbox (or the garden, if she's an outdoor sort of gal), she poops out millions of tiny parasite eggs. These hardy little troupers can survive in dirt or water for over a year, during which time all sorts of animals—including humans—can accidentally ingest them. You don't actually have to eat cat poop to get sick—simply touching your mouth with a dirty hand can suffice. Most humans are infected with *T. gondii* not by touching cat feces but by eating meat from an infected animal, such as a cow.

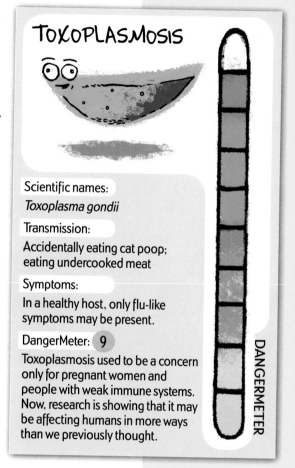

TOXOPLASMOSIS

Scientific names:
Toxoplasma gondii

Transmission:
Accidentally eating cat poop; eating undercooked meat

Symptoms:
In a healthy host, only flu-like symptoms may be present.

DangerMeter: 9
Toxoplasmosis used to be a concern only for pregnant women and people with weak immune systems. Now, research is showing that it may be affecting humans in more ways than we previously thought.

DANGERMETER

Here, kitty, kitty

Although *T. gondii* doesn't make cats sick, it can make all kinds of funky things happen when it gets into another animal. The wackiest of all is what it does to rats! See, this parasite doesn't mind being in rats, but like I said, it REALLY likes cats. Getting from a rat into a cat is pretty tricky, though, because any street-smart rat will tell you it's best to keep one's distance from feline predators.

So what's a parasite to do? *T. gondii* rewires the rat's brain to be attracted to cats! Normally, rats avoid anything that even smells like a cat. Suddenly, rats with toxoplasmosis find cat pee irresistible! They can't get enough of the stuff! This results in many more rats being eaten by cats on the prowl, and that in turn allows *T. gondii* to go home sweet home.

Insane in the brain:
how case-control studies work

By examining people's blood for antibodies to *T. gondii*, scientists have determined that in some parts of the world, as many as 80 percent of us might be infected with the kitty-loving parasite. If the bug is so good at changing rats' behavior, what could it be doing to us? The answers are surprising!

Scientists are looking for potential side effects of toxoplasmosis by doing case-control studies. In these experiments, they look at people infected with *T. gondii* (the "cases") and compare them to people of the same age and gender who live in the same area but do not have the parasite (the "controls"). If the scientists see a behavior that is much more common in the cases than in the controls, it could mean that *T. gondii* is causing that trait, although it's not proof positive.

So what have scientists found? People with *T. gondii* infections are more likely to get into potentially dangerous situations, get into traffic accidents, prefer the smell of cat pee to pee from other animals, give birth to more sons, have slower reaction times, and be more suspicious of others. There's no data on whether they like sitting in sunbeams, meowing, and chasing bits of string, though...

HELICOBACTER PYLORI— One Tough Tummy Critter

Your stomach is not a very nice place. In order to digest the food you eat, your tummy must be filled with gastric acid—a combination of hydrochloric acid, potassium chloride, and sodium chloride (better known as salt) that breaks down the proteins found in food particles.

A surprising home

Most microbes don't like acidic environments, especially one as harsh as the stomach. So for many decades, scientists assumed that our tummies were bug-free. In 1982, though, two Australian scientists named Barry Marshall and Robin Warren made an amazing discovery. When they looked under the microscope at stomach tissue from patients with ulcers and stomach inflammation, they saw tiny curved bacteria—bacteria that weren't present in tissue samples from healthy patients. They speculated that perhaps these bacteria—now known as *Helicobacter pylori*—might be the cause of the patients' tummy troubles.

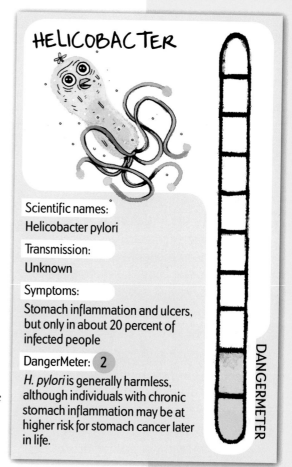

HELICOBACTER

Scientific names:
Helicobacter pylori

Transmission:
Unknown

Symptoms:
Stomach inflammation and ulcers, but only in about 20 percent of infected people

DangerMeter: 2
H. pylori is generally harmless, although individuals with chronic stomach inflammation may be at higher risk for stomach cancer later in life.

DANGERMETER

HIDING IN MUCUS

Helicobacter survives the harsh stomach environment by hiding within the layer of mucus that lines our stomach walls. It's able to sense the acidity of its surroundings, so if it accidentally strays too close to the highly acidic gastric juices, it uses its tadpole-like tail to swim deeper into the mucus layer.

FACT

Oh yeah? Prove it!

It was a great theory, but nobody believed them! The scientific community insisted that bacteria simply couldn't survive in the stomach. Finally, after two years, Barry Marshall got so frustrated with his colleagues that he decided to prove once and for all that *H. pylori* caused stomach inflammation and ulcers. What did he do? He drank it! Yup, Dr. Marshall brewed up a nice liquid culture full of *H. pylori* and chugged the whole thing.

Three days later, he began to feel sick. On day eight, a special scope was used to examine his stomach, which showed lots of inflammation—none of which was there before he drank his cootie cocktail. On day fourteen, he cured himself by taking antibiotics to kill the bacterium. And by the time he published the results of his self-experiment, the scientific community finally believed him. In 2005, Marshall and Warren received the Nobel Prize.

  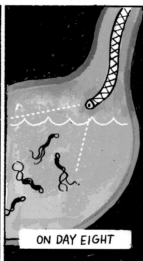 

The tummy bug family tree

Researchers have discovered that humans have been carrying *H. pylori* in their stomachs for tens of thousands of years. In fact, by building a family tree of *Helicobacter*, it was recently shown that humans were infected before our ancestors migrated out of Africa—and we've been carting this little tummy passenger around ever since.

You can even tell where a person's family came from by looking at the type of bacterium he or she carries!

H. pylori is the most common infection in the world — over half the people on Earth carry the bacterium in their stomachs!

39

Germs and Us—Together Forever

When you think about moments in history that shaped civilization, you may think of Columbus landing in America, the invention of the engine, or the two world wars. But did you know that germs have been one of the most important influences on human society?

About 7,500 years ago, humans began living together in small settlements. By 5,500 years ago, these villages had grown into larger cities—the perfect environment for germs to spread from person to person.

Where did these earliest great germs come from? Studies have shown again and again that the germs infecting humans are usually close relatives of pathogens that cause disease in animals— measles, for example, is a cousin of similar viruses in dogs and cattle. When humans began domesticating animals for use in farming and transportation, the animals'

germs suddenly became our germs, too.

Since then, humans and germs have lived side by side in a complex relationship. Epidemics of infectious diseases have wiped out whole civilizations, but they have also inspired some of the most important inventions in history: sanitation, vaccines, and antibiotics. Germs have even left their signature in our genetic code!

Living in a world full of pathogens is a constant chess game—for every move we make against the germs, they respond with a clever counterattack. For that reason, we'll probably never live in a germ-free world. Instead, our best offense is a good defense—staying one step ahead of our naughty neighbors through proper hygiene, modern medicine, and a little common sense.

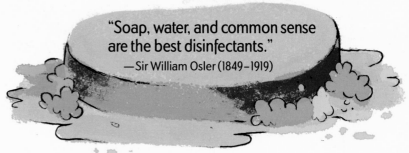

"Soap, water, and common sense are the best disinfectants."
—Sir William Osler (1849–1919)

Game Changers

Germs have changed the course of human history on many occasions — sometimes in surprising ways.

Politics and the plague

Caused by the bacterium *Yersinia pestis*, the plague has wiped out huge numbers on more than one occasion. In 541 CE, it killed as many as one in four citizens of the Byzantine Empire. The deaths weakened the Empire's armies and stalled Emperor Justinian's attempt to unite the Byzantine and western Roman Empires. If he had succeeded, today's Europe might look very different!

The plague also stopped French general Napoleon from expanding his territory. After seizing control of Egypt in 1798, Napoleon tried to invade neighboring Syria. Within days, his troops began showing signs of plague. After only a few months, Napoleon retreated, having lost as many as two thousand soldiers to disease.

Time out!

Sometimes, germs can even bring about a truce! For example, in 1995, the Sudanese government declared a two-month cease-fire in its civil war to allow health workers to visit villages, bringing with them vaccines and medications to treat parasitic diseases.

The problem with potatoes

It's not just human germs that have influenced history—a plant pathogen was responsible for one of the largest human migrations ever. In 1845, *Phytophthora infestans*—better known as potato blight—killed as many as half of the potatoes in Ireland. The potato was the major food source for many Irish, and the resulting famine forced over one million people to leave the country and make a new home overseas. Your ancestors might have been among them!

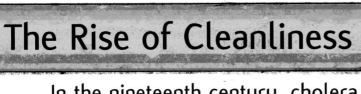

The Rise of Cleanliness

In the nineteenth century, cholera killed millions, but it also sparked one of history's greatest innovations — sanitation.

The mean and unclean streets

In the 1800s, cities were dirty, crowded places. People would go to the bathroom in chamber pots and dump the contents into the street. Human waste ran freely into rivers used for drinking water, butchers dumped rotting animal carcasses in the streets, and ruthless landlords crowded whole families into single rooms. These cramped, putrid conditions were perfect for the spread of waterborne diseases like cholera.

In 1850s London, the Thames River was full of the cholera bacterium, *Vibrio cholerae*. Outbreaks of disease happened all over the city. In 1858, the stench coming from the river was so strong that the British Parliament almost had to relocate to avoid what was being called the Great Stink of London.

Sanitation innovation

Faced with a sick and angry public, British politicians realized their only hope at cleaning up the Thames and stopping cholera was to prevent poop and other waste from reaching the river. They hired an engineer named Joseph Bazalgette to design a sewer system. It would redirect the city's sewage away from the Thames and into treatment plants, where the filthy water would be cleaned before being returned to the river.

This was the beginning of sanitation—the practice of removing trash and sewage to limit contact between humans and our waste. Cholera cases dropped in London, proving Bazalgette's sewers worked. Soon most major cities in Europe and North America had their own sewer systems.

Super sneezes and crazy coughs

How fast do germs fly out of your nose and mouth when you cough or sneeze? Coughs have been clocked at 33 feet per second (10 meters per second)—the speed of the world's fastest runners—and sneezes at an amazing 164 feet per second (50 meters per second)! Happily, stopping all this speedy snot is actually pretty simple. Use a disposable tissue when you cough or sneeze, put it in the trash right away, and wash your hands afterward. If you haven't got a tissue, sneeze into the crook of your arm instead—this keeps germs off your hands, where they can easily spread to anything you touch.

The importance of hygiene

Sanitation isn't just about toilets and sewers; it also includes hygiene—the things we as individuals can do to prevent the spread of disease. Hand-washing is one of the simplest and most effective ways of controlling disease. Be sure to lather up with soap and warm water, and scrub for at least twenty seconds—about as long as it takes to sing "Happy Birthday" twice over.

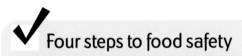

Four steps to food safety

A lot of the groceries we buy aren't as clean as we think they are. Over one-third of the packaged chicken in stores carries *Campylobacter* or *Salmonella* bacteria! That's why proper handling and preparation of foods — especially raw meats — is a must.

There are four simple steps to keeping food safe:

1. Clean!

Wash your fruits and vegetables thoroughly, and clean your cutting boards, utensils, and countertops with hot, soapy water before and after every use.

2. Cook!

Use a thermometer to make sure that meat is cooked to a high temperature all the way through.

3. Separate!

Don't allow raw meat to come in contact with other foods when you're shopping, putting the groceries away, or preparing your meals.

4. Chill!

Don't leave meat at room temperature — thaw it in the fridge, not on the countertop, and make sure leftovers are refrigerated within two hours of cooking.

Vaccines

In 1796, the smallpox epidemic led to the discovery of vaccination. Diseases haven't been the same since.

The story of one of the most important techniques in medicine starts in eighteenth-century Europe, where a deadly disease called smallpox was ravaging the population. Caused by an airborne virus called *variola*, smallpox killed almost half a million people every year. Smallpox patients were easy to spot—their entire bodies were covered in hard bumps.

In the midst of the epidemic, Edward Jenner, then only thirteen years old, was working as an apprentice to a local surgeon when he noticed something interesting. Farmers and milkmaids who had caught cowpox—a cow disease caused by a cousin to the smallpox virus—never got sick with the more dangerous human illness.

A cow called Blossom

Many years later, Jenner, now a doctor, got to test his hypothesis that cowpox infection prevented smallpox disease. A local milkmaid came to Dr. Jenner's office with a case of cowpox, contracted after she milked an infected cow called Blossom. Jenner took a small amount of pus from one of her cowpox sores and rubbed it into a cut on the arm of his first experimental subject, a young boy named James. Two months later, Dr. Jenner exposed James to a small amount of the smallpox virus. The risks were high. If Jenner was right, the cowpox James had received would protect him against smallpox. But if Jenner was wrong, James could die.

To everyone's delight, James remained healthy, showing no signs of smallpox at all! Even when Jenner exposed him to smallpox over and over, the boy never showed a hint of illness. Dr. Jenner's experiment was a grand success, and the first vaccine had been invented.

How do vaccines work?

The basic principle behind vaccination hasn't changed since Jenner's cowpox experiment—although thankfully today's vaccines are much more sophisticated than a vial full of blister pus! The idea behind vaccination is to show your body's immune system what a dangerous virus or bacterium looks like, so that if it ever sees that bug, it can quickly mount an attack and prevent infection. It's a lot like using wanted posters to warn people about criminals—when they see a picture of a bank robber or a cat burglar, folks can be on the lookout and alert police if they see the baddies around town.

"B" on guard

When you're injected with a vaccine, cells called B cells start producing antibodies. Once a B cell has seen a particular germ, it becomes a memory B cell—just like an elephant, a memory B cell never forgets. For the rest of your life, if a memory B cell sees this germ again, it will start pumping out antibodies that circulate throughout your body and latch on to the virus or bacterium. This binding prevents the germ from entering your cells and causing damage. The B cell then recruits other types of immune system cells to destroy the germ before it has the chance to make you sick.

Picture this!

How do you show your immune system a picture of a pathogen? Scientists have three tricks to train your immune cells to recognize germs. Some vaccines—like Jenner smallpox vaccine—contain live viruses or bacteria that are similar to the germ you want to protect against but that don't cause disease. Other vaccines contain the actual germ you want to vaccinate against, but the germs have been killed with chemicals, heat, or radioactivity. A third type of vaccine is made of tiny broken pieces of the germ, like the spike proteins on the outside of the influenza virus.

Antibiotics

In the early twentieth century, bacterial infections like tuberculosis caused millions of deaths every year. Scientists worked frantically to find a cure, and it was eventually discovered in a most unlikely place.

Medicine's messy marvel

Alexander Fleming (1881–1955) was a Scottish doctor on a mission. In the First World War, he worked in army hospitals, where he saw many soldiers die after their wounds became infected with bacteria. After the war, Fleming started a laboratory, where he hoped to find a cure for these deadly infections.

Fleming was a great scientist but not such a great housecleaner. Although he was well respected, his laboratory had a reputation for being a bit of a mess. A lot of a mess, actually. He'd leave Petri dishes full of bacteria all over the place and would often forget about them for weeks at a time. But as it turned out, Fleming's mess would accidentally lead to one of the greatest discoveries of the twentieth century.

The magic molecule

In 1928, Fleming came back from a long vacation and found that one of his bacterial cultures—a Petri dish full of *Staphylococci*—had been contaminated by some sort of bluish-green mold. When he looked closer, he noticed that wherever there was a fungus spot, all of the nearby bacteria had been killed!

Fleming's fungal culture turned out to be a mold called *Penicillium*. Found in soil, *Penicillium* produce a molecule called penicillin under certain growth conditions. This was the magical molecule killing the bacteria in Fleming's Petri dish.

One marvelous melon

Right away, researchers around the world began working on ways to mass-produce penicillin. It took many years. By 1942—fourteen years after Fleming's discovery—scientists had only made enough penicillin to treat ten patients! In 1943, with the Second World War under way, the need for an antibacterial drug that could be given to wounded soldiers was urgent. Researchers worked day and night to increase production…but it took a cantaloupe to save the day!

A moldy melon bought at a Peoria, Illinois, market turned out to harbor a strain of *Penicillium* fungus that produced more penicillin than researchers had ever seen. Thanks to this funky fruit, by 1944 over two million doses of penicillin had been produced. One year later, over 600 billion doses were available, and the age of antibiotics had arrived.

The ABCs of antibiotics

Antibiotic means "against life." Antibiotics are any substance capable of stopping the growth of replicating microbes, such as bacteria. But since viruses can't replicate by themselves, antibiotics won't work on them! Antibiotics do work against some fungi and parasites, but these infections are usually treated with other drugs.

Different antibiotics work in different ways. Some, like penicillin, prevent bacteria from growing, while others starve bacteria of vital nutrients they need to survive. Some antibiotics only target certain types of bacteria, while others wipe out everything they see—including the friendly microbes that live in our bodies. If you're taking antibiotics, it's a good idea to restock your body with friendly microbes. You can do this by eating foods containing bacteria, like yogurt or milk, or by taking probiotics—powders or capsules containing good bacteria.

Revenge of the Bacteria

In the relationship between humans and germs, it's a constant battle to stay on top. We discovered antibiotics, but the bugs quickly found a way to fight back.

For a while after the first antibiotic was introduced, the bacteria around us were all sensitive to the new drugs. Infections could be cured in a matter of hours, and doctors enthusiastically wrote prescriptions for the miraculous medicine. Within a few short years, however, antibiotic resistance began to emerge.

Birth of a superbug

A single bacterium developed a mutation—a change in its genetic instruction manual—that allowed it to survive inside someone who was taking antibiotics, even while all its microbial neighbors were killed. That lone bacterium divided, passing the mutation on to its children, and its children's children, and so on. Within hours, one resistant bacterium had become millions of resistant bacteria.

This happened over and over again in patients around the world. Researchers went on the hunt for new antibiotics—ones that bacteria had never seen before—but no matter what drugs they introduced, bacteria would quickly evolve resistance to the treatments. Only a few decades have passed since the first antibiotic was produced, and we now live in a world of superbugs—bacteria that have become resistant to almost every drug we have.

Jenner, Fleming, and you?

The discoveries of vaccines and antibiotics are great examples of how scientists work. When faced with an urgent problem—like a viral epidemic or millions of deaths from a bacterial infection—researchers work quickly to find a solution. Antibiotic resistance is the latest such problem, and creative scientists around the world have been inventing new ways to combat this. Who will make the next great discovery? It could be you!

Tiny spears

And that discovery might come from a surprising place…like a blister on a frog! In 1987, Michael Zasloff discovered that when the hormone epinephrine (also known as adrenaline) was sprinkled onto a frog's skin, tiny blisters would appear. Inside those blisters were millions of tiny proteins called magainins. Magainins are remarkable. Shaped like tiny spears, they poke holes in the membranes of bacterial cells. This kills the bacteria without damaging healthy cells, making magainins an exciting possibility to treat infections.

BAILING OUT BACTERIA

Bacteria have evolved many ways to outwit antibiotics, from producing proteins that can chew up antibiotic molecules to disguising themselves so the antibiotic can't lock on to its target. Some bacteria even pump antibiotics out of the cell as fast as they come in—just like bailing water out of a leaky boat!

Genes, Genomes, and Germs

Germs haven't just influenced human history—they've also shaped human biology.

Inside every one of us is a very special alphabet. This alphabet—called deoxyribonucleic acid, or DNA—spells out the instructions to make a human being. The complete set of instructions to make each of us is called our genome.

The recipe for you

You can think of a genome as a recipe for a human. And just like a real recipe, it can be broken down into steps. A cooking recipe is made up of sentences that are strings of words. Our genome "recipe" is made up of chromosomes (we have twenty-three pairs of them), and each chromosome is a string of genes (there are about twenty thousand genes in your genome). Finally, just as each word is a series of letters, each gene is a series of chemicals called nucleotides (it takes 3 billion of these to make a human). The nucleotides' full names are adenine, cytosine, guanine, and thymine, but scientists abbreviate them as A, C, G, and T.

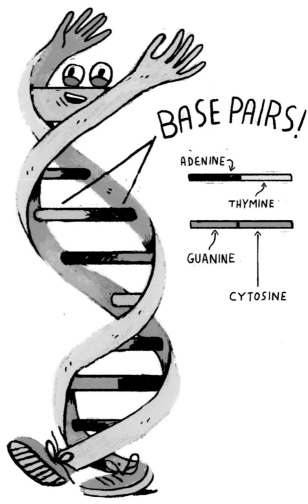

BASE PAIRS!

ADENINE
THYMINE
GUANINE
CYTOSINE

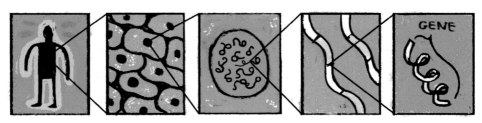

GENE

Evolution: it's in your genes

Almost everything about us is encoded in our genes. They determine physical traits ranging from eye color to how wet our earwax is to—and this is important—how likely we are to develop certain diseases in our lifetime. Our genes also determine how we respond to pathogens—some people are more susceptible to particular infections than others.

Sometimes one of our genes mutates. Let's say one of the nucleotide letters changes from an A to a C. If this mutation is beneficial—it makes us more resistant to a pathogen, for example—it will survive and be passed down to our offspring. This is called evolution. Humans evolve over very long time scales (thousands of years), but bacteria and viruses evolve quickly. This kind of evolution is what enabled antibiotic resistance to spread so quickly, and it's also what helps the influenza virus to change its disguise every year.

The genetics of protection

Because humans and germs have co-existed for so many years, our genome has evolved traits that protect us from infectious diseases. One of the most famous of these was discovered in the 1940s. The biologist J. B. S. Haldane noticed that sickle-cell anemia—a blood disease that occurs in certain families— was unusually common in tropical regions. He guessed that something about the gene producing sickle-cell anemia must be beneficial—otherwise evolution would have caused it to disappear from the population. His hypothesis was confirmed a few years later, when it was shown that this gene protected people from contracting malaria.

SMELLS LIKE LOVE

What's the most important trait in a prospective mate? Intelligence? Strength? Wealth? How about smell? Yup, smell! In several studies, women who were given sweaty T-shirts to sniff were shown to prefer the scent of men who had very different MHC genes from their own. These genes control our immune system's recognition of pathogens. The more diverse a set of MHC genes you have, the more pathogens you can recognize and fight off. Therefore, women want to mate with someone whose MHC genes are different from their own—this would give their kids the best possible immune system.

Adventures in Public Health

Concerned about cooties? Perturbed about pathogens? Bothered by bugs? Fear not—public health is on the case!

Public health is the collective name for the many individuals whose job it is to protect a population from infectious disease...and it takes a LOT! In North America, large teams of people work together to keep particular regions safe—tens to hundreds of people are needed to keep a city or a large geographic area healthy, and thousands of people are needed to look out for a whole country.

Within a public health team, there are many different experts—everyone from nurses who administer vaccinations and mathematicians who calculate how fast a disease is spreading to microbiologists who investigate pathogens in the lab.

Together, the team is responsible for:

SURVEILLANCE
keeping a lookout for any unusual disease activity

DIAGNOSIS
using laboratory tests to figure out which germ is making somebody sick

PROTECTION
making sure things like sanitation and vaccination are being used

DISEASE CONTROL
stopping outbreaks before they can spread to too many people

PROMOTION
encouraging people to adopt healthy lifestyles

Meet the Microbe Hunters

Here are just a few of the friendly folks who keep you safe from what's making people weak this week.

Epidemiologists

An epidemiologist's job is to monitor how many people are sick and which germs are going around in a given population. If an outbreak happens, epidemiologists are the ones who try to work out where the germ came from and how it spread from person to person.

Medical Microbiologists

These are doctors who specialize in identifying microbial menaces. They run laboratories that diagnose and study germs. They also design lab tests to detect new bugs.

Mathematicians

Using formulas, mathematicians and statisticians can predict how a disease will spread through a population and how effective certain control programs might be.

Sociologists

Public health isn't just for medical scientists. People who understand human behavior are also important. That way, a public health program—like an ad campaign to get people to wash their hands—will reach its audience.

Doctors and Nurses

These brave pros can often be found at the front lines. They see patients every day and are often the first people to spot a new infectious disease. They're also our key to stopping germs in their tracks—they treat patients and administer vaccines, and they are an important and trusted source of information in their communities.

Public health is an exciting field. Infectious diseases are unpredictable, so the master microbe hunters need to be ready for anything! Whether they spend their days using the internet to track people's health or chasing a sick bat through a jungle, these disease detectives never have a dull moment.

Outbreak!

When surveillance triggers an alert, the disease detectives go to work to contain an outbreak before it can spread.

Keeping count of cooties

Infectious diseases are hard to count. Imagine you were given the job of figuring out how many people in your town had a cold this week. What would you do? Call every house and ask if the occupants feel sick? Knock on every door and look for people with the sniffles? That would take a very long time, even in a small town. Now imagine trying to do that for a big city like New York or London or Toronto. Or a whole country!

To monitor the amount of disease in a population, epidemiologists use shortcuts—counting the number of lab tests being done to diagnose a particular germ, for example, or using healthcare data to track how many people are seeing their doctors about a specific illness. When they notice more reports of a disease than usual, an outbreak is declared! By talking to patients about what they did, who they saw, and what they ate in the days or weeks before they got sick, epidemiologists try to find a common link that might explain the outbreak—such as a food item that everyone ate or an event they all attended. With this knowledge, they can then find more people who might have been exposed and treat them before they fall ill.

BINGO!

FACT

SNIFFLE, COUGH, AND...CLICK?

Recently, epidemiologists have turned to a new tool to track disease—the internet. When people get sick, they often go to a search engine and type in their symptoms, trying to figure out what's wrong with them. By tracking the number of times people search for the word "flu," researchers at Google demonstrated that they can predict the level of influenza activity in a particular region.

John Snow:
the First Disease Detective

In 1854, London's Soho neighborhood was gripped by a cholera outbreak. Within ten days, over five hundred people had died from the terrible disease. John Snow, a local doctor, believed that contaminated water was behind the outbreak. After talking with some of the people in the community, he became suspicious of a public water pump located on Broad Street that many residents used as a source of drinking water.

Snow needed to demonstrate that only people using the Broad Street pump were falling ill, and he needed to work quickly—thousands of lives were at stake. He interviewed hundreds of Soho residents who had become sick (cases) and hundreds who hadn't (controls) about their activities, including their drinking habits and water sources. He found that the sick cases almost always reported using the Broad Street pump, while the healthy controls did not.

Snow's evidence convinced authorities to take the pump out of service. Immediately, the cholera cases decreased. Not only did Snow's work contain the outbreak, but the principles of epidemiological investigation he established are still used today!

GOT A SMARTPHONE? YOU CAN BE A DISEASE DETECTIVE, TOO

The HealthMap project, led by scientists at Boston's Children's Hospital, has created a smartphone app that lets you keep track of infectious disease outbreaks in your area. Their Outbreaks Near Me program scans websites looking for news reports about clusters of disease cases. It then plots them on an interactive map you can browse on your phone, letting you channel your inner John Snow.

Pandemic!

Most infectious diseases cause only small outbreaks. Every so often, though, one bug hits the big time!

Keeping count of cooties when germs go global

Epidemiologists use three words to describe the scale of an infectious disease: epidemic, endemic, and pandemic. The scale relates to not only how many people are getting infected, but where in the world the infection is happening and for how long the phenomenon is lasting. It all adds up to the difference between a disease being a big problem, or a REALLY BIG problem.

The scale of an INFECTIOUS DISEASE

EPIDEMIC
when we are seeing more cases of a disease than we would expect in a particular area

ENDEMIC
when a disease persists at a constant level in a particular region of the world

PANDEMIC
when a disease quickly spreads to every corner of the globe

Playing the pandemic game

Not every great germ is capable of causing a pandemic. For starters, a germ can't spread worldwide if a good proportion of the population already has immunity to the bug through vaccination or previous exposure. Second, the germ has to spread easily from person to person—diseases that are hard to catch, like many of those transmitted through blood, rarely cause pandemics. And third, it can't be too deadly. Diseases like Ebola are highly contagious, but because they kill their hosts so quickly, they don't have time to spread beyond a small area.

For a germ, causing a pandemic is a bit like playing Snakes and Ladders. Some moves can get it ahead in the game—like infecting someone who boards an airplane to another country. Other moves send it back to square one—like scientists developing a vaccine.

YOU WERE THERE!

The most recent pandemic to sweep across the planet was the H1N1 influenza virus in 2009. People called it the swine flu because it jumped from piggies to people.

FACT

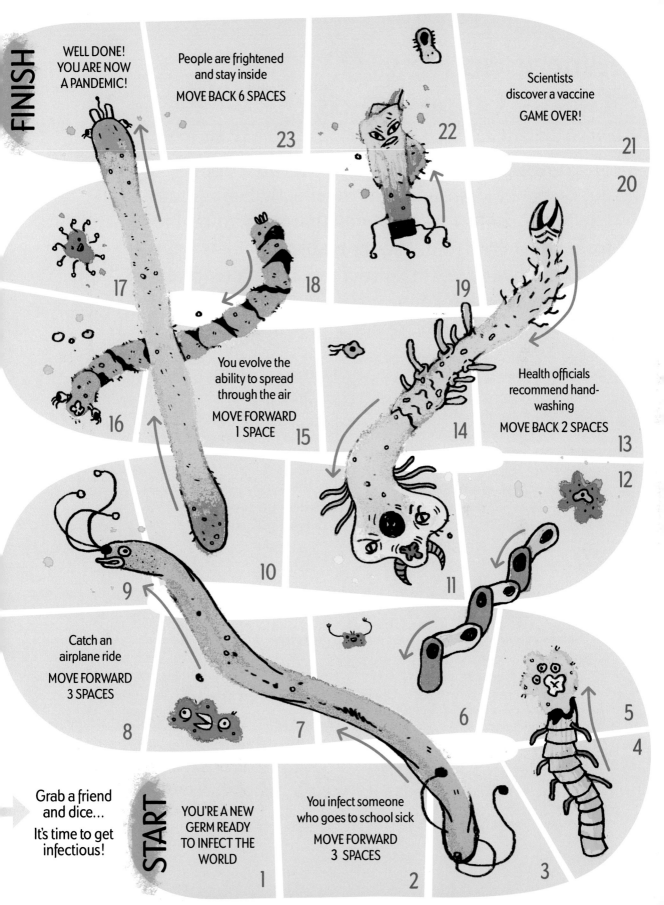

Where Do New Germs Come From?

Our surveillance systems sometimes pick up brand-new diseases, but these don't just appear out of the blue. Instead, our own activities put us into close contact with cooties that used to be hidden from humankind. Since 1940, epidemiologists have recorded over three hundred new infectious diseases, most of which are zoonoses—germs that jump from animals to humans. Here are a pair of examples.

Nipah virus

In 1999, pig farmers in Malaysia started coming down with an unusual disease. Some had trouble breathing, while others had encephalitis—a general term to describe brain swelling. Almost half of the sick patients died. Not only were the farmers sick, but so were many pigs. At first, doctors thought the pigs and their handlers were sick with a virus called Japanese encephalitis. Then they noticed that many of the sick farmers had been vaccinated against this very disease. Something much more sinister was afoot.

Researchers went to work analyzing patient samples and quickly found the culprit—a virus very similar to one discovered in horses in 1994. The new disease was named the Nipah virus after the town of Nipah, Malaysia, the home of the patient whose sample was used to discover the virus.

Disease detectives went to work trying to find the source of the virus, and it wasn't long until they had their answer:

Nipah virus is naturally found in certain types of bats called megabats (also called fruit bats or flying foxes). Normally, these bats live in the jungle, where they munch on fruit trees. Unfortunately, the bats' favorite trees were being cut down by farmers who wanted to use the land to raise pigs and other livestock. The bats would fly away, but not before pooping (unintentionally, we think) into the pigs' enclosures.

The Nipah virus, which used to stay well within the jungles where the fruit bats lived, was carried along with the bat poop into the pigpens, where it began to infect the swine. From the pigs, the virus quickly jumped to humans.

SARS

SARS stands for severe acute respiratory syndrome, and for a few months in 2003, the world was gripped with terror that this frightening new virus might be the deadliest germ since the Spanish flu that

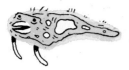

killed millions in 1918. SARS first appeared in November 2002, when a Chinese farmer died with symptoms of what looked like a bad flu. Over the next few months, more and more cases of this mystery "flu" happened in the same Chinese province.

In March 2003, cases began to appear in the busy metropolis of Hong Kong. One victim stayed in a local hotel, where he infected sixteen other people from around the world. When those people boarded planes to head home, they unknowingly brought the virus with them, causing small outbreaks everywhere from Canada to Vietnam.

Scientists worked around the clock to identify the new virus. They soon found the culprit, which they named SARS coronavirus, and quickly went to work making a vaccine. Fortunately, it didn't have to be used. After the Hong Kong outbreaks hit the news, doctors were on high alert for the new disease. When they saw a case, they knew to isolate that patient right away. This simple step stopped SARS in its tracks. It disappeared off the map in June 2003, having infected just over eight thousand people and causing 775 deaths.

Like the Nipah virus, SARS was traced back to bats. This time, it was the humble horseshoe bat. These little flyers carry the SARS coronavirus and somehow transferred it to civets, cat-like animals found in the wilds of China. Civet cats are often sold at wild-animal markets in busy places like Hong Kong, and that's how the virus was able to make the jump from cat to human.

In the wild

Together, Nipah and SARS showed that the next great germs are most likely to come from animals. As a result, researchers around the world have started to look for new diseases in wildlife, hoping to spot the next pandemic before it starts.

CONCLUSION
The End?

Thanks to hygiene, vaccination, and the marvels of modern medicine, we've been able to banish some diseases to the history books. But our future isn't germ-free...

Humans and germs will always share this planet, but with science on our side, many of us will live our entire lives with nothing more serious than a sniffle or an upset tummy. Smallpox used to be one of the deadliest diseases on Earth, but until you read this book you probably hadn't heard of it. Why? Because smallpox is the dinosaur of the disease world—it's extinct!

Getting rid of a disease—we call this eradication—is no easy feat. For a virus like smallpox, it means making sure that everyone on the planet is immune. The last recorded case of natural smallpox happened on October 26, 1977—181 years, 5 months, and 12 days after Edward Jenner administered the first smallpox vaccine. It took that long to vaccinate almost everyone in the world, leaving the smallpox virus without anyone to infect.

Public health teams are now working to eradicate other diseases— they've already eliminated rinderpest, an animal disease related to measles, and they're close to winning the battle against human diseases like polio. But for every pathogen we prevent, every cootie we control, every microbe we manage, there are hundreds more ready to take their place in The Big Book of Great Germs. Some pathogens pester our planet's population year after year and will probably be bothering us for centuries to come. Other bugs are brand-new to us, jumping into the human population as a result of changes in the way we interact with the Earth and with each other.

We're surrounded by millions upon millions of microbes, and a few of them will make us sick. It's not their fault— they're just trying to get along in the world, looking for a nice warm place to live and multiply. Sure, sometimes that nice warm place ends up being your nose or throat or tummy, but for germs, it's home sweet home.

So what's a kid to do to keep the peace with the virus or bacteria next door? Remember what Dr. Osler said over one hundred years ago: soap and water and common sense are the best disinfectants!

INDEX